D0882044

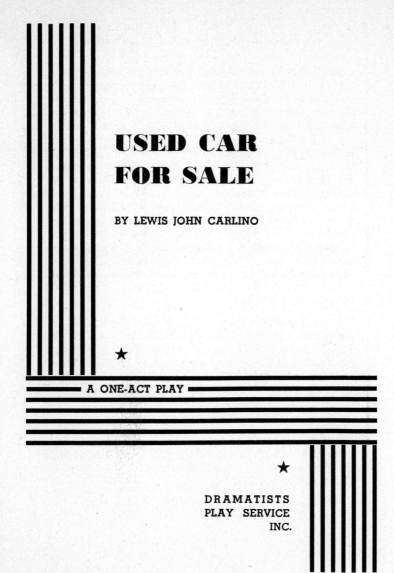

USED CAR FOR SALE

BY LEWIS JOHN CARLINO

A ONE-ACT PLAY

★

DRAMATISTS
PLAY SERVICE
INC.

SOUND EFFECT RECORD

The following sound effect record, which may be used in connection with production of this play, is available through the Play Service. The record sells for $3.25, which price includes packing and shipping.

Car engine running, car starting, driving off, approaching and stopping   No. 5041

To Elsa for smiles

CAST

CHARLIE INGERSOLL, *a young old man*

HANK SHRAVER, *a grocery clerk*

GEORGE PATMORE, *an old young man*

SUZI BRENEMAN, *a springtime girl*

SETTING

A house in the mid-west. The present.

USED CAR FOR SALE

It is mid-morning. We see the open porch of an antique house. On one side of the porch there are strings of morning glories running up to the roof. A few potted plants are scattered about. On the front railing of the porch, there is an empty flower box. On porch R., there is a caged parakeet. Next to the house, stage R., we see the rear end of a 1934 Chevrolet coupe. It is painted a bright yellow. Its presence forms a bizarre contrast to the dilapidated surroundings. On the rear fender we can see a cloth and a can of polish. There is a tarp on the ground. The door of the house opens and Charlie Ingersoll comes out onto the porch. He is a man of about seventy, with a great head of white hair. There is a youthful sensitiviness about his eyes that one cannot associate with his age. He limps to the cage with a box of bird seed.

CHARLIE. Dad gum it, Mr. Never, you are about the most eat'nist bird I did *ever* see. Wish you could have a little more consideration! Cleanin' your cage is gettin' to be a real chore. (*Filling cup.*) You know what day this is? Why, this is Sunday. This is visitin' day! Yes, siree, I bet we get at least two callers from town today. Only one last week. Can't really count that though, what with all that wind kickin' up that dust. Sure was nice of that gentleman to come out here in all that wind. You know what, Mr. Never? With all this here sunshine and the sky lookin' big and clear like it does, I bet we have *more'n* a couple of callers. Yes, sir, nothin' like a big sky and sunshine for callin' on people. Kinda makes ya feel big; like ya wanna stretch your legs across the whole countryside. You know when I . . . (*Looks toward the car.*) Doggone, I forgot the wax can on Desdemona. (*Walks from porch to car, picks up can and cloth, and looks at car af-*

fectionately.) Yellow. (*Turns and shakes his fist at the parakeet.*) I don't care what folks think! That's her personality and that's the color she'll be! People always puttin' their two cents in. Why, when my sister Helen's kids lived in town, lord bless her soul, they could see me and Desdemona comin' a mile from King's Point. They'd stand up on the roof of that porch and yell, "It's a yella one! I can see it! It's a yella one. Here comes Uncle Charlie and Desdemona!" (*He chuckles.*) Knew I'd give a nickel to the first one that saw us. (*Pauses and looks wistfully at the horizon.*) Funny how kids grow up inta bein' people, then die and move away. It's a wonder how that happens. People always puttin' their two cents in! (*Shakes his fist once more at the parakeet.*) She ain't never gonna be no color but yellow! You mark my words, bird! (*He smiles in anticipation.*) Gettin' late. Better change my shirt if we're gonna have company. (*Charlie takes the can of polish and walks up the porch and into the house. A moment passes and Hank Shraver, a town grocery clerk, enters from R. He is a man in his middle twenties. There is road dust on his clothing. He walks to the porch steps and sits for a moment. He places the newspaper he has been carrying on a step and mops his brow with a handkerchief. Looking up, he spies the car. He gets up and walks to it. Deciding to test the springs, he jumps on the bumper and begins shaking. Being satisfied he jumps down and starts kicking the rear tires. Charlie comes out of the house buttoning his shirt.*) Hey, what you doin' there?
HANK. Just testing the tires. Best way to test a tire is to kick it. That'll tell you whether it's defective or not. Best way in the world to tell a weak casing.
CHARLIE. Why, you drugstore mechanic, who ever told you that?
HANK. Nobody ever told me. Just figured it out. Plain logic. Law of physics. You apply a strain to a weak point. If that point is weak enough, it'll go.
CHARLIE. 'Bout the only weak thing around here is your brain. Whata you mean by comin' out here and kickin' the tires on a man's car?
HANK. You Mr. Ingersoll?
CHARLIE. That's me.
HANK. Came about your ad in this morning's *Clarion*.
CHARLIE. Oh.

6

HANK. This the car?

CHARLIE. Yes, that's the car all right. (*Begins digging in flower box.*)

HANK. Sure is a long way to come from town to look at a car. Must be half a mile from the highway bus stop to here.

CHARLIE. Three-quarters.

HANK. Well, like I said, it's a long way.

CHARLIE. Yes, it's a long way. (*He begins reading a seed packet.*)

HANK. How long you had the car, Mr. Ingersoll?

CHARLIE. Bought her new, down in Carothersville, spring of '34.

HANK. One owner, huh?

CHARLIE. Only one.

HANK. How's she on oil?

CHARLIE. (*Reading.*) "Make hole about two inches deep. Drop seed in and . . ."

HANK. How's she on oil?

CHARLIE. Come up here a minute, son. My eyes ain't what they used ta be. What's this last part here?

HANK. (*Walking up on porch.*) Whata you want?

CHARLIE. Read that last part. Been a while since I planted Mornin' Glories. Wanna make sure I do it right.

HANK. (*Looks at Charlie a moment, then reads off seed packet.*) "Drop seed in a cover firmly with soil. Water generously with watering can. Do not use hose, as the pressure will dislodge seeds."

CHARLIE. That all it says?

HANK. That's all.

CHARLIE. Seems like it oughta say more'n that. Anybody could figure out that much. Don't have to go to all that trouble to print it.

HANK. The car use much oil?

CHARLIE. You ever plant any Mornin' Glories, son?

HANK. No.

CHARLIE. That's bad. People oughta plant somethin' in their lifetime. Sweet peas, Mornin' Glories, somethin'. You ever plant *anything*?

HANK. No. I work in a grocery store.

CHARLIE. You sell seed in that store?

HANK. Yes.

7

CHARLIE. And you never planted any?

HANK. No.

CHARLIE. Huh!

HANK. About the car . . .

CHARLIE. Desdemona.

HANK. Huh?

CHARLIE. The car, that's her name. Desdomona.

HANK. Well, about Desdemona . . .

CHARLIE. Yes, sir, I been plantin' things all my life. You take this here seed now, that I just pushed into the dirt. You know that seed could lay in that paper envelope a man's whole lifetime and never come to life! Kinda like something screamin' ta get born. Just you imagine now all the seeds in all the grocery stores all over the country, all over the world, just screamin' ta get born! It ain't right that a man should go through life and never plant somethin'.

HANK. I guess it's ok, if a person has time to putter around like you do. But some people have to spend their time working.

CHARLIE. Workin'? Son, there ain't no work in the world that ever kept a man from helpin' a thing grow. Why, that was the first great work a man ever had. Yes, sir, pushin' a little "be-be" of a thing into the hot ground and sweatin' over it till it grew under his hand. Hand me that water can, will ya?

HANK. What?

CHARLIE. There on the railin'. (*Hank picks up water can.*) You take like these here Mornin' Glories. In a few days why, they'll be pushin' up their little sprouts lookin' for the sun. Then they'll climb up that string higher and higher, and all along the way they'll be bustin' loose with blossoms. And all because I tore open this envelope. (*Hank stands awkwardly with the water can.*) Well, go ahead!

HANK. Huh?

CHARLIE. Put some water on 'em, they're waitin'. (*Hank tips the water can and sprinkles the flower box carefully.*) Easy does it. There now, don't that make you feel good?

HANK. Oh, yah, sure.

CHARLIE. Now you *really* been part of somethin'!

HANK. (*Puts down can irritably.*) Look here, Mr. Ingersoll, I came out here to look at that car you advertised for sale.

CHARLIE. Desdemona!

8

HANK. Well, then, Desdemona.
CHARLIE. Yep, mighty fine car.
HANK. Well?
CHARLIE. Well what?
HANK. Well, I came to look at it.
CHARLIE. *Her.*
HANK. (*Point of exasperation.*) *Her!*
CHARLIE. There she is. Look all you want. (*Hank moves to car.*) Mind you now, no kickin'. (*Charlie sits in a rocking chair on the porch and lights his pipe.*)
HANK. (*Out of sight in front of car.*) How's she on oil?
CHARLIE. Don't use a drop.
HANK. Brakes ok?
CHARLIE. Stop anytime you want her to. (*To Mr. Never in lower key.*) Sometime even when you don't want her to. Eh, Mr. Never? (*He chuckles.*)
HANK. Ever have any trouble with the radiator?
CHARLIE. Don't ever recollect none. Damn, he's a fussy one, ain't he? It appears to me like he just don't trust us, Mr. Never.
HANK. (*In sight now at rear of car.*) Tail pipe's rotted.
CHARLIE. (*Leaning back in his chair.*) Things get old. (*Quietly to himself as Hank continues his inspection.*) Yes, that's a wonder how things get old. Car and houses and memories. I guess there ain't a man alive ever figured out the mystery of that. You take and cogitate on that, Mr. Never! Me and that grocery clerk'll live our lives and then get planted in some field and just turn out to be fertilizer for some plants. Now that's economy for you! Nothin' wasted. (*Chuckles at a new inspiration.*) Hey now, wouldn't it be downright humorous if Mr. Grocery Store Clerk there turned out to be fertilizer for a patch of Mornin' Glories? (*He laughs louder.*) And him never plantin' a seed! (*His laughter grows.*)
HANK. (*Becoming aware.*) What's that?
CHARLIE. I said you and me are just gonna turn out to be two big manure piles!
HANK. What?
CHARLIE. Nothin'. Ain't important.
HANK. (*Approaching porch steps.*) Your ad says you want a hundred and fifty dollars for her.
CHARLIE. That's what it says.
HANK. That's a lot of money for a 1934 automobile.

9

CHARLIE. Yep, that's a lot of money.

HANK. You drive her much?

CHARLIE. Not for six months. Sheriff took my license away. Said I was gettin' too feeble. You ever hear such nonsense in your whole life? If I live till votin' time that tin star bureaucrat is gonna be surprised, he sure is. No, I just start her up every day and keep her polished. Car like that's like a woman. Gotta pay 'em heed or they'll go to pot.

HANK. Can I start her up? I want to hear the engine.

CHARLIE. Key's in her. Had her goin' this mornin'. (*Hank gets into car and starts engine. It runs smoothly. Charlie listens for a moment, smiling.*) Pretty, ain't it, Mr. Never? (*Engine runs a moment more, then is turned off. Hank gets out and moves to porch.*)

HANK. Sounds ok.

CHARLIE. There ain't nothin' wrong with that car, son.

HANK. I'd like to take it for a drive out to the highway.

CHARLIE. What for?

HANK. Why, I'd like to test it out before I buy it.

CHARLIE. Test it for what?

HANK. Mechanical defects. Maybe she wobbles on the road.

CHARLIE. She don't wobble.

HANK. Well, the clutch and gear shift and brakes. I want to see if they work all right.

CHARLIE. Maybe you didn't hear me right, son. I said the car was in good condition. And when Charlie Ingersoll says something about Desdemona, it's true. Maybe he lies about other things, but not with Desdemona.

HANK. I didn't say you were lying.

CHARLIE. Don't have to! Car stays right here.

HANK. How do you expect people to buy the car if you don't let them try it out?

CHARLIE. Faith, son, plain old faith. You know that's good for some folks. I ain't met any lately, but there's some it's good enough for.

HANK. What if she breaks down?

CHARLIE. Well, I figure that's her pre-rog-a-tive. Ain't much a man can do about that.

HANK. That's taking a big chance.

CHARLIE. (*Looking at Hank closely.*) Say, son, don't you ever talk about nothin' else?

HANK. Whata you mean?

CHARLIE. Ever since you come here, all you been talkin' about is Desdemona. You ain't said another word about nothin' else.

HANK. What is there to say? I mean . . . well, that's what I came out here for and . . . what else is there to talk about?

CHARLIE. (*Shaking his head.*) I guess you wouldn't understand even if I spelled it out for you. Just ain't like it used to be.

HANK. I'll give you a hundred and twenty-five. I think that's being generous seeing as how I'm just taking your word about the mechanical condition. Besides, I'll need the extra twenty-five for the paint job.

CHARLIE. What are you talkin' about?

HANK. You don't think I'm gonna drive around town in a yellow car that shade?

CHARLIE. What's the matter with that shade of yellow?

HANK. Why, you just stick out. People can see you coming a block away.

CHARLIE. They can see you a *mile* away!

HANK. That's what I mean. How'd it look if I drove up to the grocery store in that yellow thing?

CHARLIE. (*His anger mounting.*) *Thing?* I drove that car since 1934 and she's always been that shade of yellow.

HANK. Well, that might be all right for you, but my car is not going to be yellow. I won't have people laughing at me.

CHARLIE. Desdemona is *not* your car!

HANK. I'm buying her, aren't I? I guess I can change the color if I want to.

CHARLIE. (*Approaching Hank.*) You hear him talkin', Mr. Never? Now you listen to me. Anybody that buys Desdemona is gonna drive a yellow car and exactly that shade of yellow, because that's what she is. And furthermore, *you* ain't buyin' her. You don't have enough money to buy her! Anybody that'd even think about changin' her color ain't fit to have her. I knew you couldn't buy her the minute you kicked those tires. You know what I think, boy? I think you better get off my property. (*He advances menacingly.*)

HANK. Now just a minute, old timer. (*Backing away.*)

CHARLIE. Don't you "old timer" me. Get offa my property!

11

HANK. You can't do this!

CHARLIE. I don't know anybody that's got a better right.

HANK. (*Making a fast exit* R.) You're out of your mind. You're crazy! I'll report you. You wait and see. I'm gonna report you!

CHARLIE. (*In pursuit.*) Go on, git! Get offa my place! (*At extreme stage* R. *he shakes his fist.*) I wouldn't sell Desdemona to anybody that never planted a seed in his life, anyway! (*He turns and walks up the porch steps to the cage.*) Well, Mr. Never, (*Chuckling.*) how'd I do? I just can't figure out some people. Now you take . . . (*He looks stage* R.) Well, I'll be doggoned. Here comes another one! What'd I tell ya? This here is gonna be a *real* visitin' day. Ain't even noon and we got two already. (*He sits in the rocker and begins reading the paper he has picked up from the step. He hums lightly, assuming an air of nonchalance. We hear the sound of a car approaching. The engine stops and Charlie looks up from his paper to* R., *in the direction of the sound. We hear a car door slam and see George Patmore enter. He is a thin man, about forty. His movements are quick and nervous. George is a chronic worrier. He straightens himself out and walks to the porch steps, taking a newspaper from his jacket pocket.*)

GEORGE. Mr. Charles Ingersoll?

CHARLIE. Yes, sir. What can I do for you?

GEORGE. My name is George Patmore, Mr. Ingersoll. Did you place this ad in the King's Point *Clarion?*

CHARLIE. (*Getting up and walking down the steps with outstretched hand.*) Pleased to meet you, Mr. Patmore. Yep, that's my ad. Pretty, ain't it? (*He opens the newspaper he holds to the ad section and reads.*) "Used car for sale. Excellent condition. A bargain at one hundred and fifty dollars. Charles Ingersoll, Box 46, Route Two." One hundred and twelve figures and spaces. (*Shows George the paper.*) See the name there? "Charles Ingersoll." Had 'em put it all in capitals so it would stand out. Kinda distinguished lookin', don'tcha know? The part about the bargain was my own idea too. Kinda makes the ad look a little more professional. People like that, ya know? Gotta have a good forward approach when you're sellin' somethin'. (*He looks at George suspiciously.*) You here 'bout the car, I suppose.

GEORGE. Well, in a way, yes, I am.

CHARLIE. Yep, I sure am pleased to meet you, Mr. Patmore.

(*He extends his hand for another handshake. George does also. Charlie withdraws his hand leaving Mr. Patmore with his hand awkwardly extended in space.*) Damn, I'm gettin' forgetful. Already did that, didn't I?

GEORGE. (*Embarrassed.*) Er . . . yes.

CHARLIE. Say, I bet you're all hot and thirsty from that ride out here. Let me get you some lemonade.

GEORGE. No, that's quite all right. I . . .

CHARLIE. Now it's no bother at all. Got it all fixed up, settin' in the ice box. (*He starts for the house door.*) You make yourself comfortable. I'll be right back. (*He indicates two old chairs on the ground in front of the porch.*)

GEORGE. But I really don't wa . . .

CHARLIE. Be right back. (*Charlie goes into the house. George shakes his head and moves to the chair. He dusts it off with the paper he carries, and sits. He surveys the yard while impatiently tapping the paper on his knee. After a moment, Charlie comes through the door with a pitcher of lemonade on a tray. He looks down at the tray.*) Woops, forgot the glasses. (*He enters the house once more. Patmore's impatience grows. Charlie comes out beaming.*) Got 'em now. Ain't sanitary for two people to drink outa the same pitcher. 'Specially in the summertime. (*Comes down to table and places the tray and two glasses on it. He then pours.*) Something friendly about lemonade, don't you think? (*George's unspoken word is cut short.*) I wonder now how many town people sit outside and drink lemonade in the shade and talk to one another. You know, Mr. Patmore, I think that's become a lost art. I remember my sister Helen's back yard. The whole place was covered by the lace of Eucalyptus shadows. Beautiful, just beautiful. You got a back yard?

GEORGE. No. My wife and I live in a court.

CHARLIE. Yep, that cement sure covers up a lotta God's grass. You know it's a funny thing though, Mr. Patmore. I remember once when I visited Carothersville. Boy, now *there* is a place with a lot of cement. Why, I was walkin' along the sidewalk one day and happened to look down and do you know what I saw? (*George shakes his head.*) Well, right between these two cracks where the cement was joined, there was a tiny blade of grass growin'. Now ain't that a wonder? Now you just imagine that little seedlin' layin' under all that rock and pushin' up through

13

a space of what you might call mic-ro-scop-ic. Boy, that's the spirit of livin' things for ya! And do you know that . . . Well, listen to me go on. Dadgum, I just went and monopolized the whole conversation. Seems like you been waitin' to say somethin'.

GEORGE. It's about this ad, Mr. Ingersoll.

CHARLIE. Ah, yes, mighty fine car.

GEORGE. I'm sure it is, but . . .

CHARLIE. Well, there she is. Look her over if you want.

GEORGE. That won't be necessary.

CHARLIE. Do you know I've had that car since 1934? Couldn't tell that by lookin' at her now, could you?

GEORGE. Mr. Ingersoll, that isn't why I came. I don't want to buy your car.

CHARLIE. (Stunned.) You don't? But you said the ad . . .

GEORGE. I work for the King's Point Clarion, Mr. Ingersoll. I'm in charge of classified ads.

CHARLIE. Oh, well, I can save you a lot of trouble, Mr. Patmore. I mailed that last payment for the ad yesterday. Should be in your office tomorrow. No delivery on Sunday, ya know?

GEORGE. I'm not here about the payment. (He takes out a small notebook.) Mr. Ingersoll, you've been using our classified service for about five weeks.

CHARLIE. Three full months today. I remember 'cause I placed it exactly two months after the sheriff took away my license. That figures exactly three months.

GEORGE. Mr. Ingersoll, my office has, in the past month, received complaints from the following people. (Reads off notebook.) Mr. Thomas Kinic, Mr. Silas Dedmond, Mrs. Olive Guptil, and Mr. Joseph Allyson.

CHARLIE. That so?

GEORGE. (Continuing.) Ahem. Three of these people: Mr. Kinic, Mr. Allyson, and Mr. Dedmond state they agreed to pay you the price you asked, but you refused to sell. The fourth, Mrs. Guptil, says you didn't even allow her to make an offer, but just flatly refused to even talk about selling the car.

CHARLIE. Damn, and she was such a nice lady too! Never thought she'd do a thing like that. Never can tell a tattletale though, eh, Mr. Never? (George turns and looks around.)

GEORGE. The same thing apparently seems to have happened

today. The gentleman I passed on the road told me you refused to sell him the car too. Then he said something very strange. He said if I had never planted Morning Glories, I would be wasting my time talking to you about the car. (*Charlie laughs.*) This is not to be taken lightly, Mr. Ingersoll. This is a very serious matter.

CHARLIE. 'Course it is.

GEORGE. It seems, Mr. Ingersoll, that you have been misrepresenting yourself in the King's Point *Clarion.*

CHARLIE. I don't see what all the fuss is about. I send you the payments, don't I?

GEORGE. The payments have nothing to do with it! It's a matter of principle!

CHARLIE. Since when did principle have anything to do business? A horsetrader is a horsetrader whether he's sellin' cars or classified ads.

GEORGE. (*Shocked.*) Mr. Ingersoll!

CHARLIE. Oh, come off your high horse, Mr. Patmore. What's the harm?

GEORGE. What's the harm? Mr. Ingersoll, the King's Point *Clarion* has stood for veracity for the past 120 years. It cannot be associated with fraudulent advertising. If you advertise your car for sale, you must have intention to sell.

CHARLIE. Well, I do have intention to sell. I just ain't found anybody fit enough ta buy yet. Seems to me your paper just don't reach the right people.

GEORGE. Our paper reaches 64% of the population of King's Point. Statistics show that . . .

CHARLIE. Hang statistics! You ain't reachin' the good 36%. That's the failure of your paper. That's your fault not mine, Mr. Patmore.

GEORGE. (*Becoming more worried and agitated.*) Mr. Ingersoll, I did not come here to argue about the circulation of my newspaper. I repeat, the King's Point *Clarion* can have nothing to do with fraudulent advertising.

CHARLIE. Oh, it can't, eh? Well, I wanna show you something, Mr. Patmore. I been lookin' over this here paper of yours this mornin' and I wanna show you somethin'. (*Picks up newspaper and begins thumbing through pages.*) Now, let's see. Where did I see that? Nope, musta been back further. Yes . . . yes . . .

here it is. Take a look at that ad, Mr. Patmore. I want you ta read me what it says.

GEORGE. *(Reluctantly takes paper and begins reading.)* "Sale, sale! Fire sale! Forced to sell. Kirstein's Department Store offers a sacrifice savings on men's underwear. All sizes; brief and boxer types. Sale, Sale! Fire Sale! Forced to sell!" Well, what about it?

CHARLIE. I been readin' your paper now for three months and I don't ever remember havin' read about Mr. Kirstein's Department Store catchin' fire. Did he have a fire recently?

GEORGE. Well, I don't know, but I'm sure it . . .

CHARLIE. And I haven't heard or read anything about Mr. Kirstein goin' bankrupt or anything like that either. He ain't goin' bankrupt, is he?

GEORGE. I don't think so. That's not the point. He . . .

CHARLIE. Well, if he didn't have a fire and he ain't goin' bankrupt, how come he's forced to sell his underwear? That's fraudulent advertising to me, and he even does it with a bigger space than I do!

GEORGE. Mr. Ingersoll, I'm sure that if Mr. Kirstein advertises a fire sale he must have had a fire *some place!* And as far as the word "forced" is concerned, this is part of advertising jargon that is used apart from the usual meaning we give to the word.

CHARLIE. Now, Mr. Patmore, are you tryin' ta tell me the people of King's Point are gonna understand what you just told me just from lookin' at Mr. Kirstein's underwear ad? You know them people. They take a man at his word.

GEORGE. What I'm *trying* to tell you is that unless you really have intention to sell your automobile, the paper must cancel your ad.

CHARLIE. Dad gum it, Mr. Patmore. I don't see what harm it does!

GEORGE. We have the integrity of the paper to think of for our subscribers.

CHARLIE. Well, I'm a subscriber too. I can't figure it does any harm to use your classified to get a few folks out here to talk to once in a while.

GEORGE. So that's it! You have no intention at all to sell that car!

CHARLIE. Look, Mr. Patmore, what's a few calls? Why, I bet

16

you get more complaints than that every hour. Heck, that's part of the newspaper business.

GEORGE. (*Exasperated.*) The King's Point *Clarion* cannot be used as an instrument to waylay innocent townspeople!

CHARLIE. Damn it, some of them people *need* waylayin'. (*Quietly.*) I'm sorry. Dad gum it, shouldn't pop my kettle that way. (*There is an embarrassed moment of silence between them.*) I'm an old man, Mr. Patmore, but I'm not old inside. You know what makes people old inside. Loneliness, Mr. Patmore, plain bitter loneliness. Listen! You hear anythin'?

GEORGE. No.

CHARLIE. That's what I mean. I sit up on that porch all week listenin' to the countryside. Sometimes the wind comes down outa the mountains behind King's Point and rustles the tall grass out there. That's a sound, but there ain't much human comfort in it. Sometimes a jay'll perch up in that Pepper tree, but I never have been able to understand jays. I know folks think I talk too much when they come out here. Fact is I talk all the time, even when I'm alone. I guess it's just to hear the sound of a human voice out here in all this quiet. You know sometimes when the wind is rustlin' out there in the evenin' and I'm sittin' up on the porch, I can hear my sister Helen's kids scamperin' around and arguin' about the ice cream I brought them. Sometimes, it sounds so real, I shout back to them. Then the sound of my own voice covers up the rustlin' and I know where I am and who I am. Can't get into town no more. It's my leg. Can't seem to get that clutch to the floor board any more. 'Sides don't want to go in even if I could. Lot of cement goin' in King's Point from what I hear. Well, that's the way it is, until Sunday and the paper comes out. Then I get my visitors and things is better. (*His emotion rising.*) Don't ya see, Mr. Patmore? It ain't right for a man to just sit and talk to the grass. A man's gotta hear the sound of voices and people laughin' and gettin' mad. He's gotta put a glass of lemonade on the table and sit back and joke and argue. That's the only thing that'll keep a man from growin' old inside. (*He gets up and walks to the cage.*) This here bird ain't much help. (*Turns to hide his emotion.*) Man at the pet shop guaranteed he'd talk, too. Gettin' so you just can't trust . . . (*He turns suddenly and faces Patmore. There are tears in his eyes.*) Mr. Patmore, you just *can't* cancel my ad.

17

GEORGE. I'm sorry. (*With difficulty.*) I'm sorry, Mr. Ingersoll, but I have to. It's not me you understand. Those complaints have to be forwarded to the front office. I'd lose my job.

CHARLIE. Couldn't you just lose the complaints? I bet if I talked to them people, they'd see it my way.

GEORGE. They'd only call in again if your ad kept running. I'm sorry, Mr. Ingersoll. It can't be done. The complaints have to be turned in.

CHARLIE. (*Rubbing his nose on his sleeve.*) Well, I guess you have to do what you have to do.

GEORGE. I hope you understand. . . . I . . .

CHARLIE. (*Broken.*) Oh, sure, sure. (*There is another embarrassed silence.*)

GEORGE. What'll you do?

CHARLIE. (*Struggling to be light.*) Oh, don't you worry none about me. I can get along without the ad. Why, I'll just fix me up a big bright sign and take it out to the highway. Yes, sir, you'll see. There'll be cars stoppin' here from every state in the union to see me and Desdemona and Mr. Never. (*Walks to stage* R. *near the car.*) Factory workers and fishermen and their vacations, and tailors, and mechanics that'll appreciate her. All sorts of people'll be comin' up here. And we'll sit in the shade and talk and drink lemonade and maybe even dream a little. Heck, I don't need no classified ad, Mr. Patmore.

GEORGE. (*After another moment of silence.*) I . . . er . . . I better be going. (*He gets up and walks past Charlie and turns.*) I . . . er . . . good-bye, Mr. Ingersoll.

CHARLIE. (*Quietly, looking at Desdemona.*) Good-bye, Mr. Patmore. (*George exits* R. *We hear the sound of the car starting and driving off. The lighting gets darker. Charlie sees the growing shadows on the ground and looks up into the sky.*) Looks like we're gonna have some rain, Mr. Never. Sky ain't as big as it was this mornin'. Funny how the weather changes like that. Yep, can feel that water in the air already. Better cover up Desdemona. (*He picks up a tarp from the ground and covers the car. He crosses and comes downstage and picks up the tray and the pitcher of lemonade. He looks at the two glasses on the table, shakes his head, places the glasses on the tray and returns to the porch. Before he goes into the house he stops near the cage.*) Guess I better change my shirt, eh, bird? (*He enters house. A moment passes and Suzi Brenneman, a girl of 18, enters from* R. *eating an apple. There is a newspaper tucked in the back pocket of her jeans. Suzi has the irrepressible aura of springtime and youth about her. Her hair is in a pony tail. From the way she walks and moves, we know that Suzi is one of those people who never lacks of speech or curiosity. She looks around and walks to the porch.)*

SUZI. *(Yelling.)* Hello. Anybody home? *(No answer.)* Anybody home?

CHARLIE. *(Coming out of the house buttoning his shirt. We see it is the old one he had on earlier.)* Quit that screechin', I heard ya.

SUZI. 'Scuse me. I didn't mean to get you outa bed.

CHARLIE. Wasn't in bed. Just changed my shirt.

SUZI. Oh.

CHARLIE. *(Gruffly.)* Whata you want?

SUZI. You Mr. . . . Mr. . . . Just a minute. *(Takes the paper from her back pocket and thumbs through till she finds the classified section. She locates the ad and looks up.)* Mr. Charles Ingersoll?

CHARLIE. Yes.

SUZI. *(Rolling paper up and replacing it.)* I can't remember names so good. I looked at that ad three times on the bus coming out here and still couldn't remember. My aunt says that's bad. About not remembering names, I mean. You know, like John Brown, and Adams, and Marconi, and Socrates? I never could remember any of those names in school. Now that I'm out, they all come back. But I still do have trouble though. Like just now.

CHARLIE. Scrawny thing like you outa school already? You're no bigger'n a minute.

SUZI. *(Proudly.)* Uh huh. Graduated last month. Got a job at the library in King's Point. Three days a week at my Aunt Denise's and three days at the library. Help things out, don't you think?

CHARLIE. Huh?

SUZI. I mean like at home. With expenses and all.

CHARLIE. *(Sitting on porch step.)* I suppose so.

SUZI. *(Offering apple.)* Wanna bite?

CHARLIE. No, thank you.

SUZI. I think it's a girl's duty to help out at home. A girl's folks put out money for three years so she can go to high school and then what happens? Why, most girls up and get married. And all

19

that education's gone to waste! All they'll do the rest of their natural lives is make babies. Just like a factory. Just crank 'em out like nuts and bolts. All that education gone to waste. You know what I'm gonna do, Mr. Ingersoll? I'm gonna take and read a book a day from that library the rest of my life and never make any babies, *ever!*

CHARLIE. (*Absently.*) You'll change your mind in a year or two.

SUZI. (*Vehemently.*) Never! I will never! Well, I don't really mean never. I might. I just might. (*She begins scratching her back. Not being able to reach the spot, she moves to the porch railing and begins rubbing her back on it. Charlie feels the vibration and looks at her.*)

CHARLIE. Whata you doin'?

SUZI. Got bit by a horsefly swimming yesterday. Don't seem to wanna stop itching.

CHARLIE. Come over here. (*Suzi crosses and stands with her back to Charlie.*) Where?

SUZI. On the right.

CHARLIE. (*Begins scratching.*) Here?

SUZI. Little to the left more.

CHARLIE. Here?

SUZI. Up a little . . . wait . . . right there. (*Charlie scratches vigorously.*) Ah, gee, that's good. (*Playfully*) Thank you kindly, sir. (*She looks at the apple core in her hand.*) Say, I bet your parakeet would like this apple core. Can I give it to him?

CHARLIE. Sure. Mr. Never'll eat anything. Fact that's all he does do. Just eats and dirties up the cage. Got no other purpose in life but that.

SUZI. Mr. Never? What a funny name. How come you call him that?

CHARLIE. (*Warming.*) I tried to get that bird to talk for three months. Done just like the pet store man told me to. Three times a day I'd stand in front of that cage and say, "Polly want a cracker?" Three months of nothin' but cold stares. One day I just lost patience and yelled at him. "You dang bird, ain't you never gonna say nothin'?" I says. He opened up his mouth and said, "Never." That's all, just "Never." Only time he ever talked. Hasn't said a word since. Just sits there and eats. Guess I musta scared him or somethin'.

SUZI. (*In hysteria falls into rocking chair and begins rocking wildly. Charlie smiles faintly.*) Oh, Mr. Ingersoll, that's about the funniest thing I have ever heard in my natural life.

CHARLIE. Truth though. Bird's just like a lotta people I know. (*Suzi still laughs violently.*) Well, it ain't that funny!

SUZI. (*Vainly trying to control.*) Oh . . . oh. I'm sorry, Mr. Ingersoll. (*She holds her stomach.*) I just can't help myself when I get tickled like this.

CHARLIE. You oughta try ta control yourself.

SUZI. (*Her laughter quieting slightly.*) I'm trying, Mr. Ingersoll.

CHARLIE. (*Grumpily.*) What ya come out here for anyway, just ta laugh at me?

SUZI. (*Stops laughing abruptly.*) Oh, no, Mr. Ingersoll. (*She walks to Charlie.*) I hope you don't think that. I wouldn't laugh at you for the world. I like you. I come out about the car you advertised.

CHARLIE. You did, huh?

SUZI. Yes.

CHARLIE. Well, her name is Desdemona. She's bright yellow. She's in good condition. Hundred and fifty dollars, take it or leave it!

SUZI. You're spoofin' me.

CHARLIE. Don't you call me no spoofer, little girl.

SUZI. Why, you are *too*. There isn't a car in the whole world that's bright yellow and that's named Desdemona.

CHARLIE. I tell you there is!

SUZI. (*Playing with him.*) Now, Mr. Ingersoll. I certainly wouldn't say that you're fabricating or anything like that but . . .

CHARLIE. (*Getting up in a rage.*) Dad gum you, girl, I tell you there is! (*He walks to the car.*) You get down here and look if you don't believe me. (*He rips the tarp off Desdemona. There is a moment of silence in which Suzi stands wide-eyed. Charlie turns with the tarp in his hands.*) Well?

SUZI. (*Ecstatic.*) Oh, Mr. Ingersoll, she's *beautiful!* (*She walks to the car.*) Never in a hundred years, in a hundred countries could you ever find a yellow car named Desdemona. It's like . . . well, it's like a fairy tale.

CHARLIE. (*Trying to hide his pleasure.*) Didn't believe me, huh?

SUZI. (*Touching the fender with her finger.*) It's the brightest yellow I ever saw in my natural lifetime.

CHARLIE. (*Wistfully.*) Yep, she sure is pretty.

21

SUZI. *Pretty?* Why, she's downright elegant. Desdemona. She's like a fine high class lady all fit out for a ball. All shining and bright.
CHARLIE. You like her, huh?
SUZI. Oh, I surely do. Just wait'll they see me in town. I'll drive right up to the library and honk the horn. Has it got a horn?
CHARLIE. Yep.
SUZI. Well, I'll drive right up to the front steps and honk the horn three times. And everybody'll come out and look. And I'll just sit there like this, (*Assumes a supercilious pose with hands on the wheel.*) and never say a word. Just like this! And they'll walk around and around and never believe there ever was a car like Desdemona. And I'll just sit there like it was a common ordinary every-day-like-thing. And Miss Potts will come down to look too. She's the librarian. And I'll say, "Good morning, Miss Potts. I *drove* to work this morning. Miss Potts, I'd like you to meet Desdemona. Desdemona, meet Miss Potts." Then I'll honk the horn like Desdemona was saying "Howja do." And Miss Potts'll stick up her nose and turn around and walk back up the steps and I'll say, "I'll be right in soon as I park her." And best of all, they'll be nobody sniffing at my rhubarb pies.
CHARLIE. What?
SUZI. We like rhubarb pies at our house. Ma bakes 'em twice a week and I have to take 'em over to Aunt Denise's on the bus, when I go over to mind the kids. Seems like everybody gets mad at me when I get on the bus with them hot rhubarb pies. Bus driver said I hadn't oughter get on the bus during lunch time. Said it isn't fair to the riders. Seems like he has trouble seein' out the back when people move over to sit close to me. There isn't anything in the world like the smell of hot pies. You like 'em, Mr. Ingersoll?
CHARLIE. It's been a long time.
SUZI. That's what I mean. How many people still make rhubarb pies? Mr. Ingersoll, you know what? Next time we bake, I'm going to bring you a couple.
CHARLIE. I'd like that. Certainly has been a long time. Say, why don't you call me Charlie?
SUZI. Yes, I think that would be nice. Oh, won't it be wonderful going to work and over to my Aunt Denise's in Desdemona, Charlie? Taking the kids for picnics and rides! Oh, there'll be all kinds

of wonderful things to do and see with her. (*She stops suddenly with a worried look.*) Mr. Ingersoll . . . er . . . Charlie . . , I've got twenty dollars.

CHARLIE. What?

SUZI Oh, now don't get mad. I'll be able to pay for her. She's worth every bit of a hundred and fifty too. Yes, sir, every bit. It'll just take a while, that's all.

CHARLIE. (*Picking up the scent.*) How long you figure?

SUZI. Well, let me see now. I work three afternoons at the library for three dollars. That's nine dollars. I get a dollar each afternoon at my Aunt Denise's. That's three more. Nine and three is twelve. Give Mom seven. You think seven a week is fair?

CHARLIE. I guess so.

SUZI. Ok, so I give Mom seven. Keep three out for gas. That leaves two. I can make it two dollars a week until the balance is paid up. Payments every Sunday, never fail.

CHARLIE. (*Smiling.*) That'll take a long time.

SUZI. (*Seriously.*) Oh, but she's worth it!

CHARLIE. If you was to . . . (*A car is heard coming up the road stage* R. *The horn sounds and the car comes to a stop. We hear the door slam.*) Why, that looks like Mr. Patmore comin' back.

SUZI. (*Worried.*) Does he want to buy the car? (*Charlie doesn't answer.*)

GEORGE. (*Entering breathless from stage* R.) Mr. Ingersoll, it's about your ad again.

CHARLIE. (*Approaching him.*) You look in terrible shape, Mr. Patmore. Come right over here and sit down. (*He leads Patmore over to the chair and helps him into it.*)

GEORGE. Oh, thank you. I do believe I've had a palpitation this morning. Oh, this is terrible! (*He wipes his brow with handkerchief.*)

CHARLIE. Now calm yourself down a minute. What's this about the ad?

GEORGE. Well, right after I left here, I became confused about my decision. Seeing as how this has never happened in the history of the paper. That's one hundred and twenty years you know.

CHARLIE. I know.

GEORGE. Well, I called the editor and explained the whole situation, about the car and your disability and all. He told me that

23

it would make a wonderful story. He wants to release it to all the major papers. Then he said if I wanted to keep my job that I should come back out here and make sure you kept the ad in. He's even authorized me to offer you the ad free of charge.

CHARLIE. You mean things can be just like they was? I can have my ad and keep Desdemona?

GEORGE. (*Eagerly.*) Yes . . . yes.

CHARLIE. I don't know now . . .

GEORGE. It means my job, Mr. Ingersoll. Think of that. What'll my wife say?

CHARLIE. Things just like they was, eh?

GEORGE. Exactly.

CHARLIE. (*Looks at Suzi who stands expectantly, then back to Mr. Patmore. He delivers his line on turning back to Suzi once more.*) I'm sorry, Mr. Patmore. Desdemona has just been sold. (*Suzi looks up. Her face is exploding with happiness.*)

GEORGE. But, Mr. Ingersoll, you just can't sell Desdemona!

CHARLIE. Already did! Don't you worry none about your job now. It wasn't your fault the sale was made. Story's just as good now as it was. You tell your editor to come out and see me. I'll explain the whole thing to him. Can't have fraudulent advertising in the King's Point *Clarion,* now can we?

GEORGE. (*Smitten.*) No, sir. (*He gets up slowly.*) Well, goodbye, Mr. Ingersoll. (*He walks stage* R. *Suzi has moved to Desdemona.*

CHARLIE. Good-bye. (*Before he is offstage.*) Oh, Mr. Patmore. I suggest you get another job. One you can feel a little more secure in. Ain't right for a person to worry like you do.

GEORGE. Thank you. I'll think about it. (*He exits* R. *We hear the sound of the car start up. Charlie climbs the porch steps and waves as the sound diminishes.*)

CHARLIE. (*Waving.*) Good-bye. Come back again.

SUZI. (*Waving also.*) Good-bye.

CHARLIE. (*Looking at sky.*) Looks like it might not rain at that. (*Looking* R.) You know with that story comin' out, I bet we have all kinds of people out here. Maybe with all that jabberin' Mr. Never'll learn to talk. (*Looks at Suzi.*) Ahem, now about this sale. I think we got some considerin' to do about price. There's a tail pipe that'll have to be replaced. I guess we can make some allowance for that. And then there's . . . Say, girl, would you like a glass of lemonade?

SUZI. (*Coming to the step.*) Why, Charlie, I'd just *love* a glass of lemonade.

CURTAIN

PROPERTY PLOT

Potted plants
Empty flower box
Parakeet in cage; cup in cage
Chevrolet coupe, old model, bright yellow (only rear is seen)
Cloth and can of polish (for car)
Box of bird seed
Packet of seeds
Newspapers
Pitcher of lemonade on tray
Glasses
Tarp on ground
Apple

New

TITLES

I NEVER SANG FOR MY FATHER
THE PROMISE
DR. COOK'S GARDEN
COMPULSION
SATURDAY NIGHT
IT'S CALLED THE SUGAR PLUM
DEAR FRIENDS
APPLE PIE
MINOR MURDER
HE TO HECUBA
THE BRIDE'S BOUQUET
RATS
JONAH
BALLOON SHOT

● *Write for information*

DRAMATISTS PLAY SERVICE, INC.

440 Park Avenue South   New York, N. Y. 10016

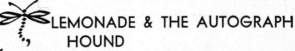

NEW

Plays

THE WRONG WAY LIGHT BULB
AN ORDINARY MAN
ZELDA
THE SERPENT
SWEET EROS & WITNESS
MICKEY
HEY YOU, LIGHT MAN!
A WIND BETWEEN THE HOUSES
THE MADNESS OF LADY BRIGHT
THE TEN O'CLOCK SCHOLAR
AMERICAN ROULETTE
BIG MOTHER

New
PLAYS

A CRY OF PLAYERS

DOES A TIGER WEAR A NECKTIE?

THE DOZENS

ADAPTATION

MARATHON '33

STOP, YOU'RE KILLING ME (Three Plays)

GREAT SCOT! (Musical)

IVORY TOWER

A LIMB OF SNOW & THE MEETING

SATURDAY ADOPTION

THE PASSING OF AN ACTOR

MISS FARNSWORTH

DRAMATISTS PLAY SERVICE, Inc.

440 Park Avenue South   New York, N. Y. 10016

RECENT

 *Releases* . . .

JIMMY SHINE
IN THE BAR OF A TOKYO HOTEL
THE GINGHAM DOG
MISTER JOHNSON
SCANDAL POINT
TEA PARTY & THE BASEMENT
THE PEOPLE NEXT DOOR
THE STRONG BREED
THE TRIALS OF BROTHER JERO
FRIDAY NIGHT (Three Plays)
THE FLOUNDER COMPLEX
WINE IN THE WILDERNESS

Write for information as to
availability